Distance & Tasks Chart

Area: _____

Date: _____

Distance (feet/meters) / Tasks

www.enna.com
www.productivitypress.com

Distance & Tasks Chart

Area: _____   Date: _____

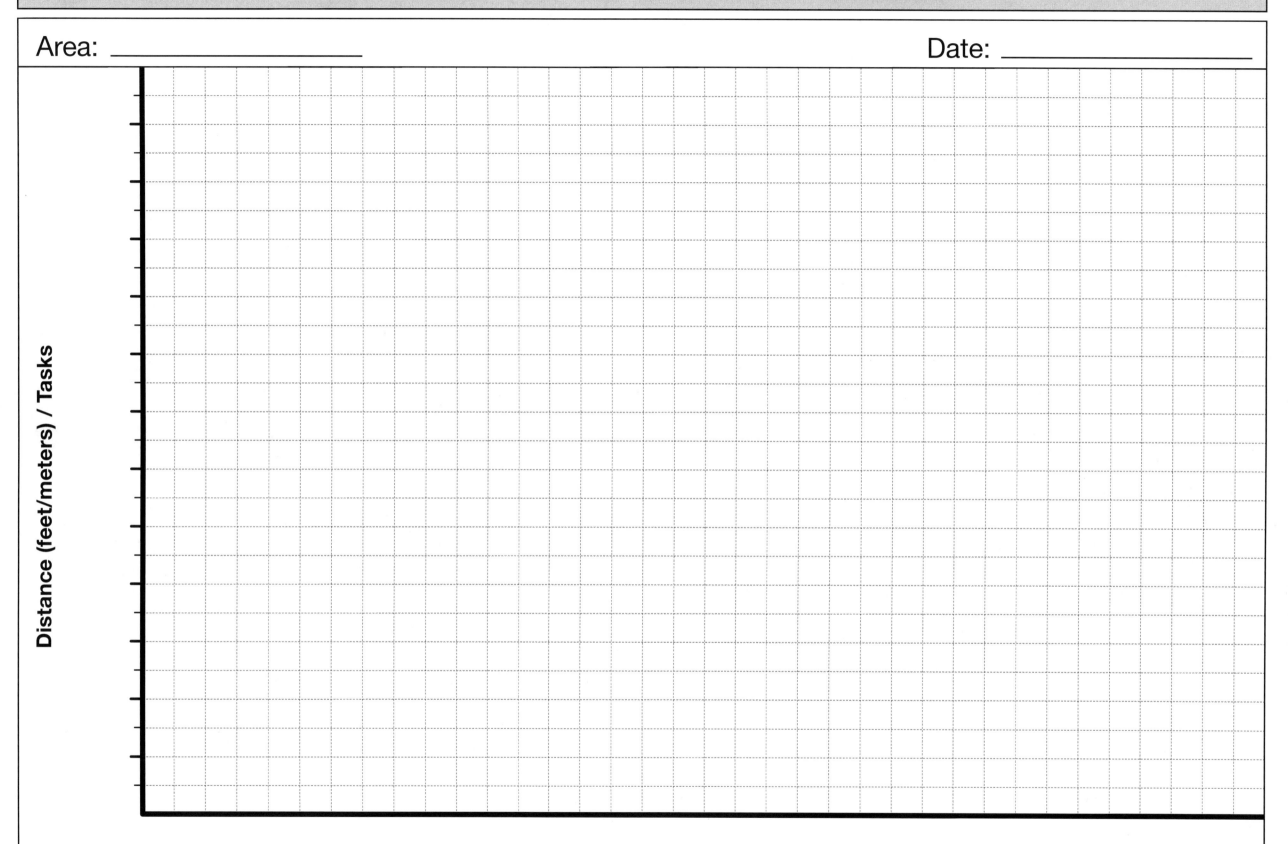

Distance (feet/meters) / Tasks

www.enna.com
www.productivitypress.com

Distance & Tasks Chart

Area: _____   Date: _____

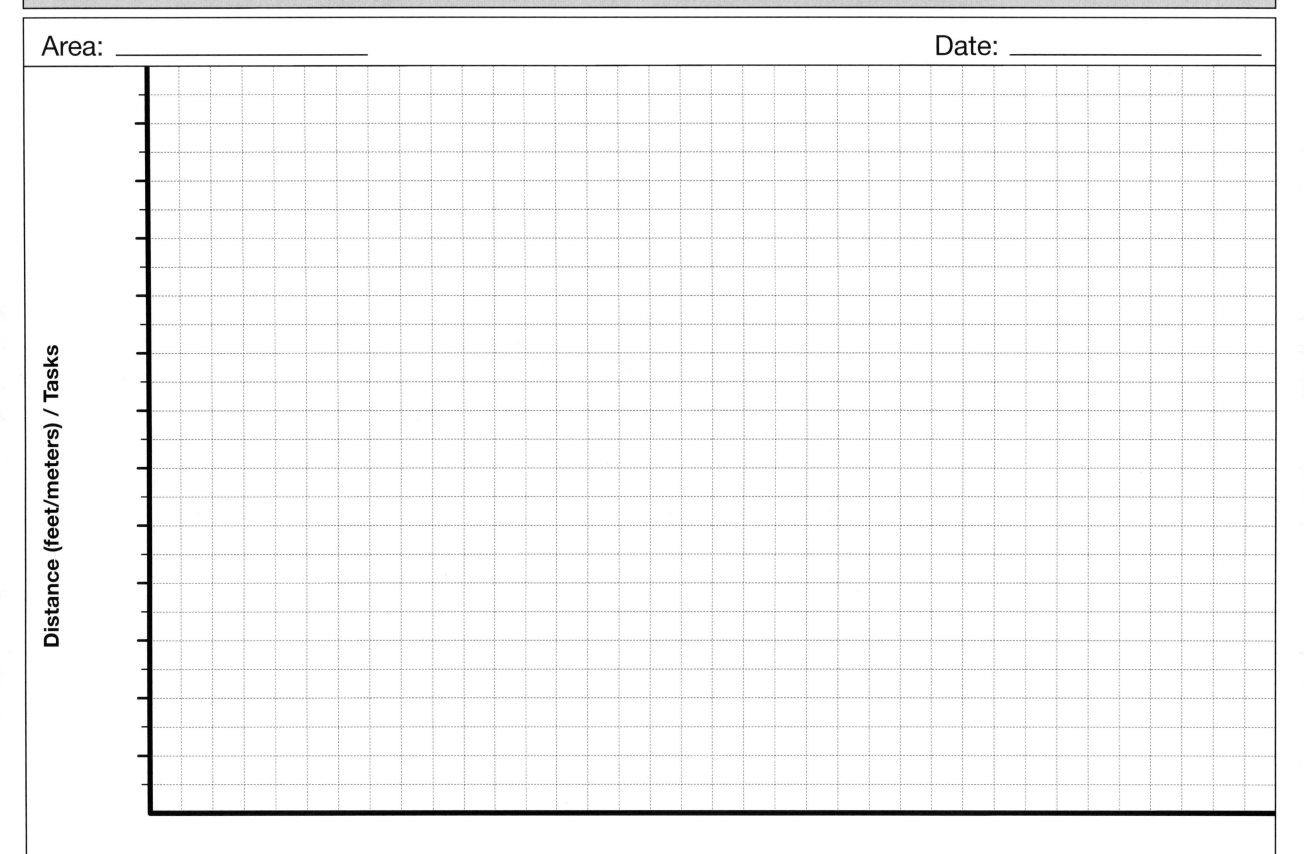

Distance (feet/meters) / Tasks

www.enna.com
www.productivitypress.com

Distance & Tasks Chart

Area: _____   Date: _____

Distance (feet/meters) / Tasks

Distance & Tasks Chart

Area: _____   Date: _____

Distance (feet/meters) / Tasks

www.enna.com
www.productivitypress.com

Distance & Tasks Chart

Area: _____   Date: _____

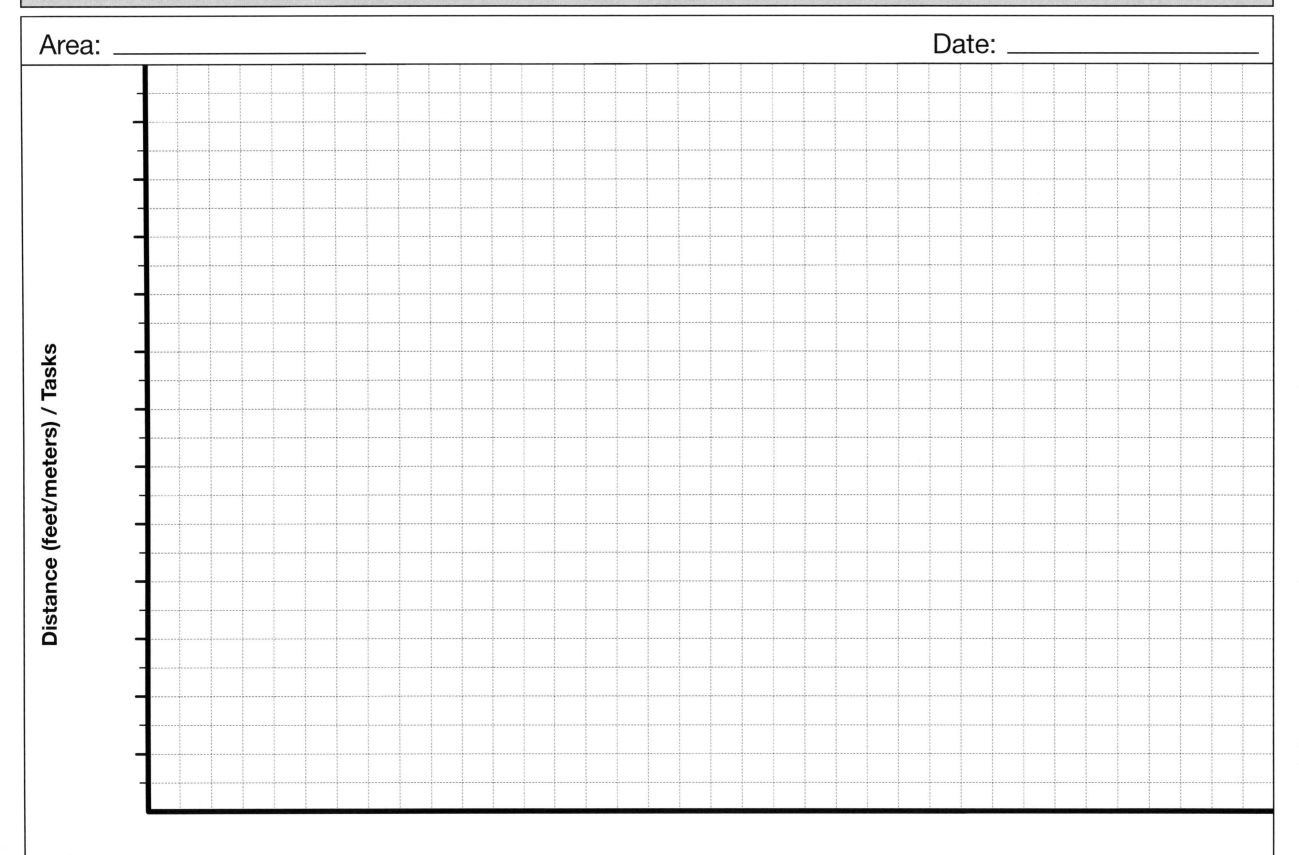

Distance (feet/meters) / Tasks

Distance & Tasks Chart

Area: _____   Date: _____

Distance (feet/meters) / Tasks

www.enna.com
www.productivitypress.com

Distance & Tasks Chart

Area: _____   Date: _____

Distance (feet/meters) / Tasks

Distance & Tasks Chart

Area: _____   Date: _____

Distance (feet/meters) / Tasks

www.enna.com
www.productivitypress.com

Distance & Tasks Chart

Area: _____   Date: _____

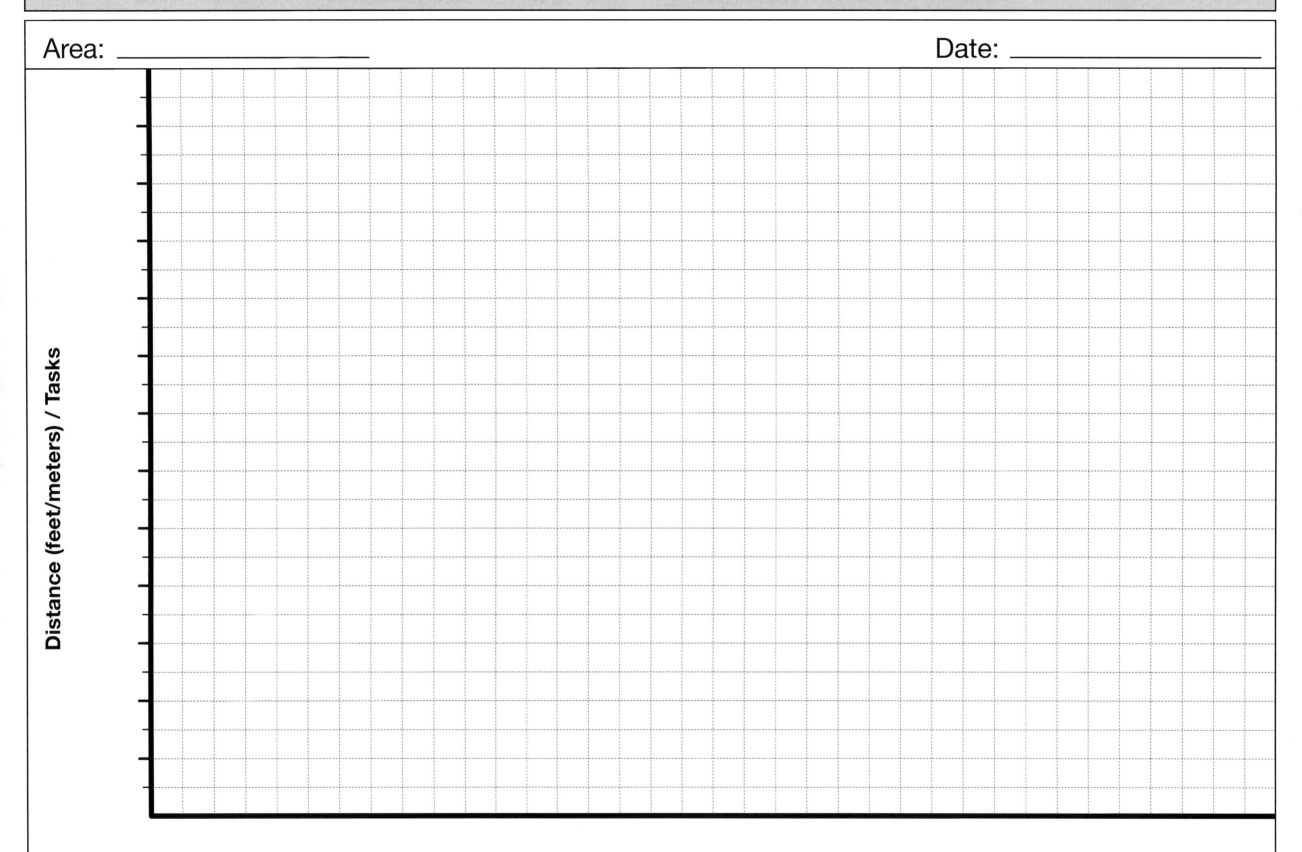

Distance (feet/meters) / Tasks

Distance & Tasks Chart

Area: _____   Date: _____

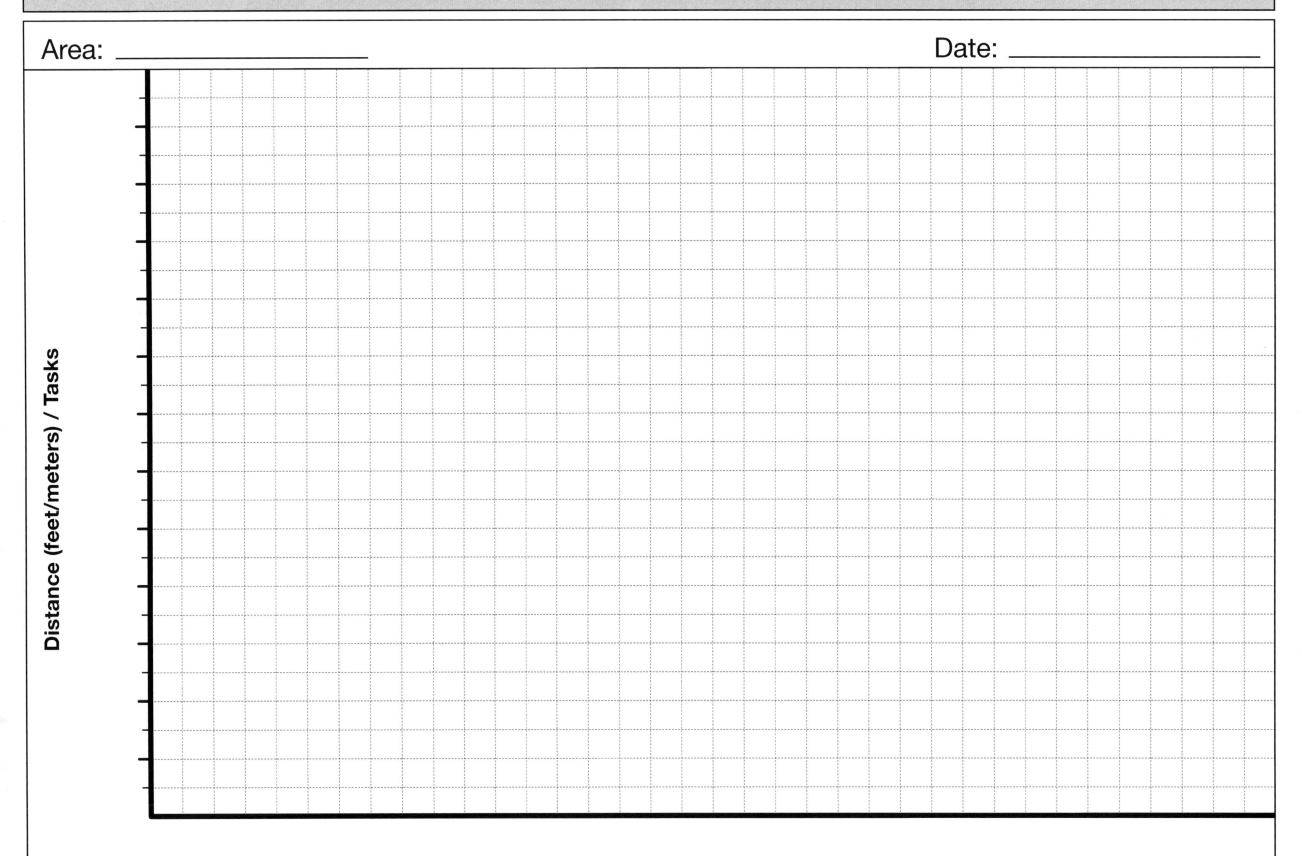

Distance (feet/meters) / Tasks

www.enna.com
www.productivitypress.com

Distance & Tasks Chart

Area: _____   Date: _____

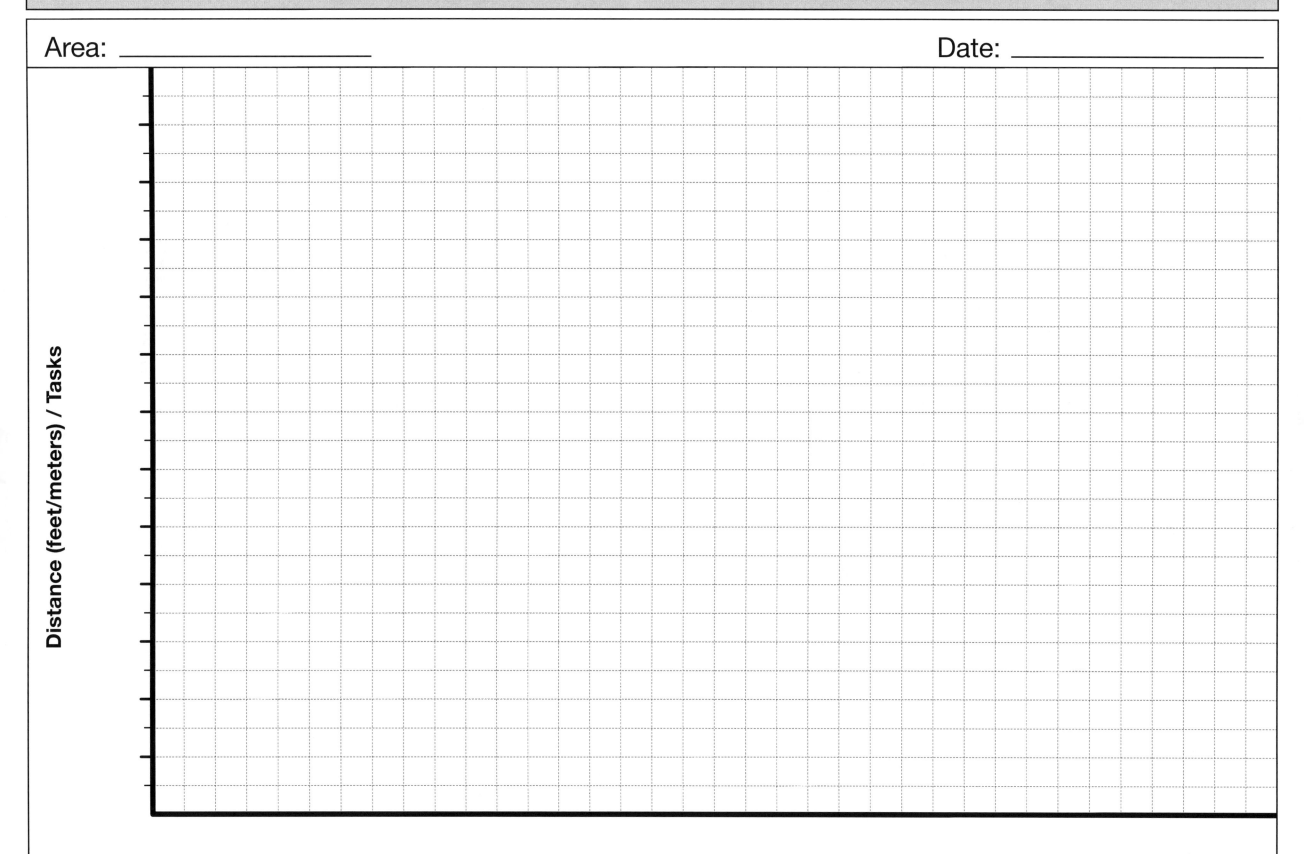

Distance (feet/meters) / Tasks

Distance & Tasks Chart

Area: _____   Date: _____

Distance (feet/meters) / Tasks

KNOWLEDGE INTO PRACTICE

www.enna.com
www.productivitypress.com

Distance & Tasks Chart

Area: _____   Date: _____

Distance (feet/meters) / Tasks

www.enna.com
www.productivitypress.com

Distance & Tasks Chart

Area: _____   Date: _____

Distance (feet/meters) / Tasks

www.enna.com
www.productivitypress.com

Distance & Tasks Chart

Area: _____   Date: _____

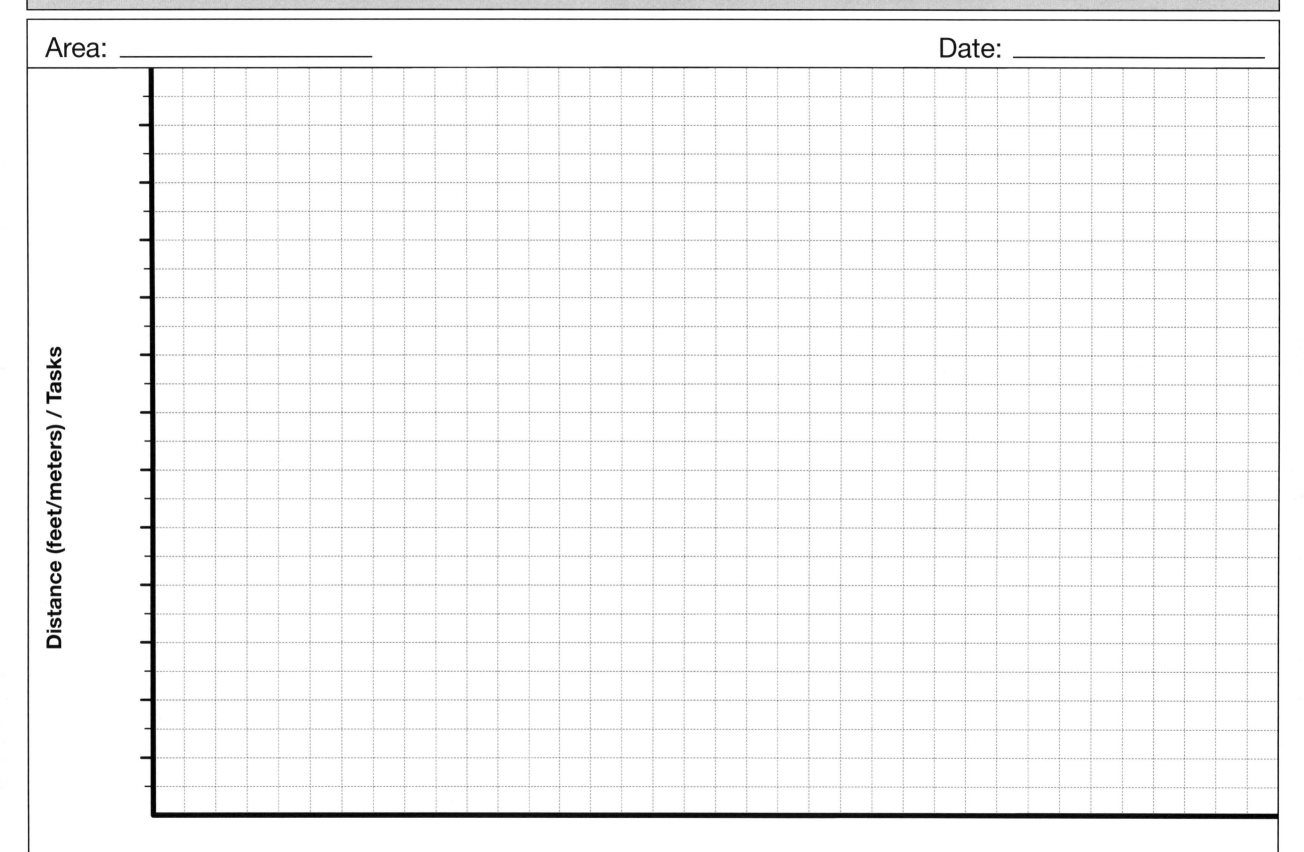

Distance (feet/meters) / Tasks

Distance & Tasks Chart

Area: _____   Date: _____

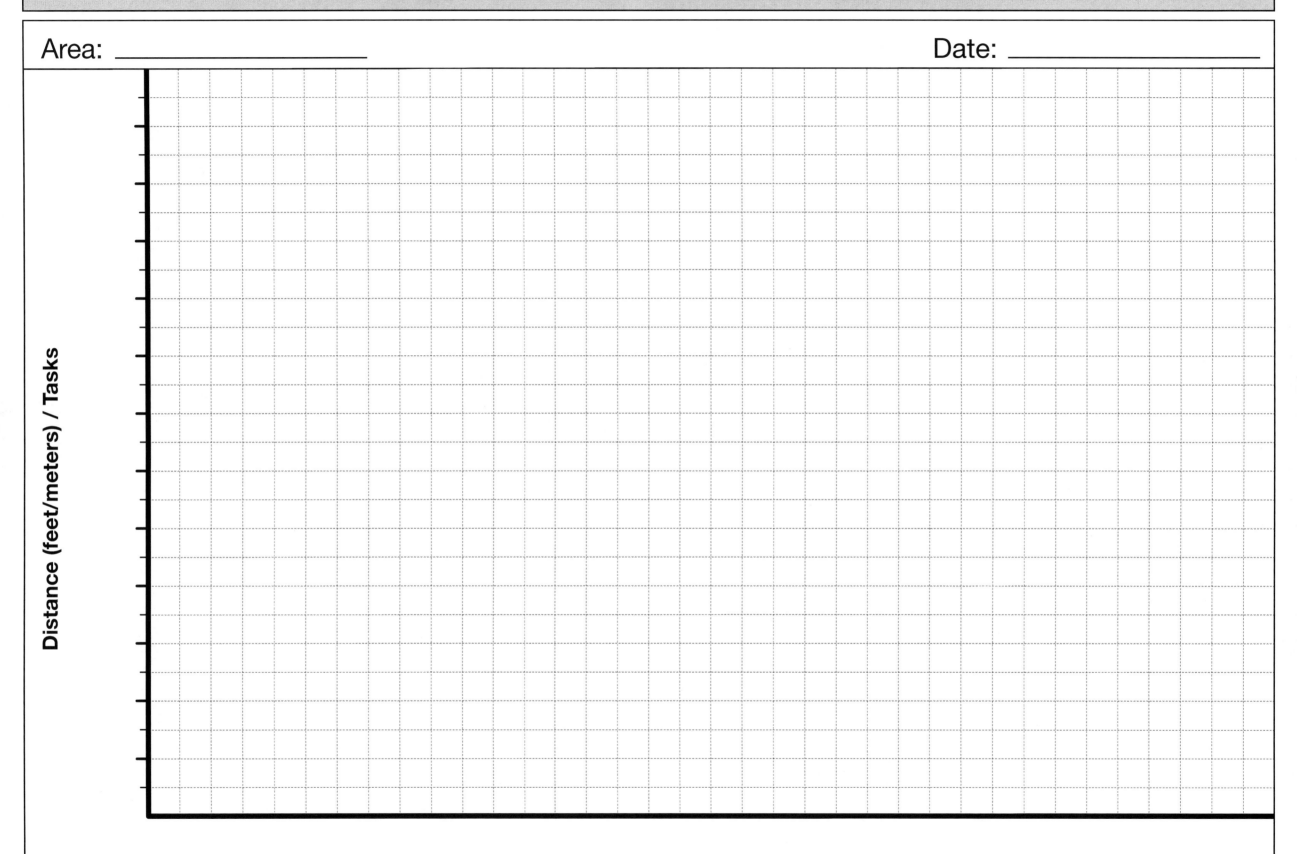

Distance (feet/meters) / Tasks

www.enna.com
www.productivitypress.com

Distance & Tasks Chart

Area: _____   Date: _____

Distance (feet/meters) / Tasks

www.enna.com
www.productivitypress.com

Distance & Tasks Chart

Area: _____ 　　 Date: _____

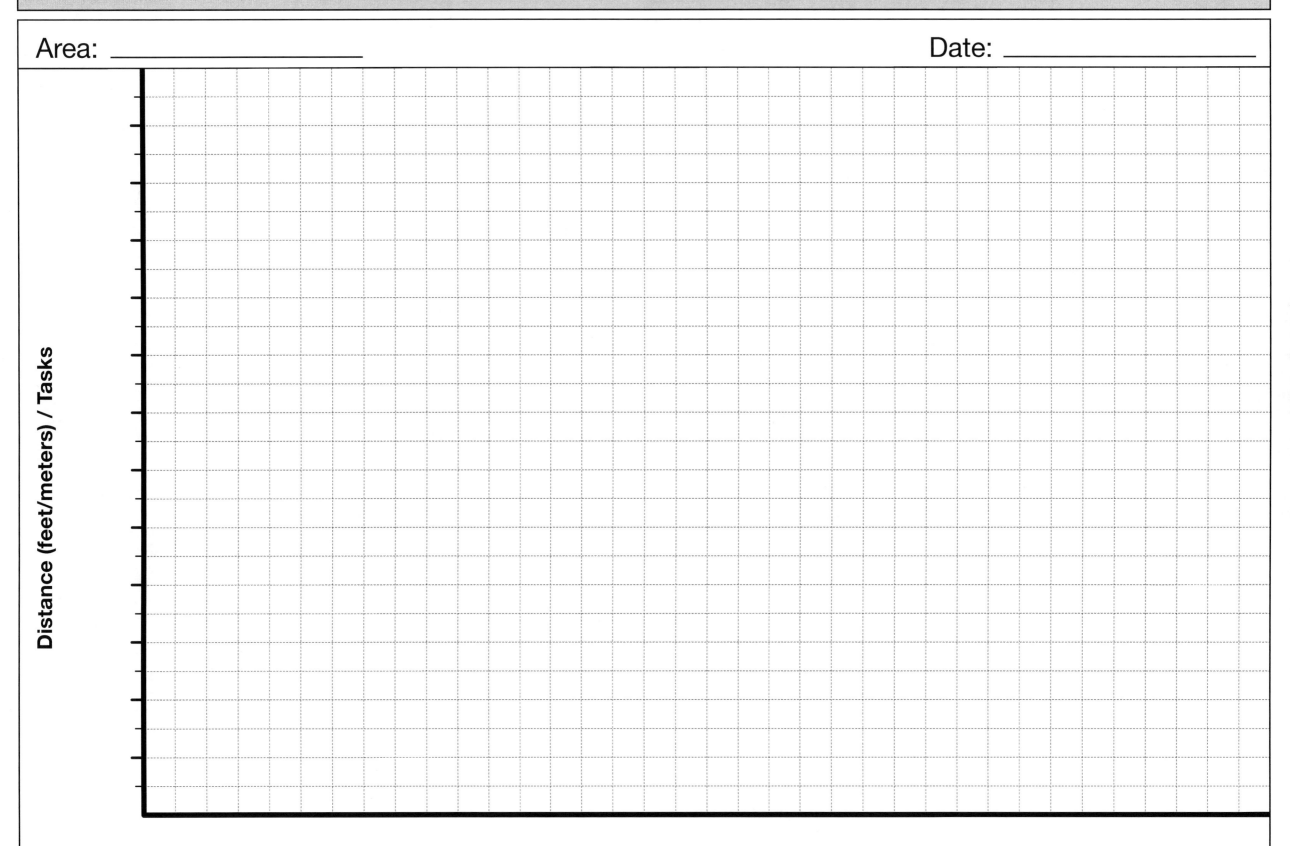

Distance (feet/meters) / Tasks

_____

www.enna.com
www.productivitypress.com

Distance & Tasks Chart

Area: _____   **Date:** _____

Distance (feet/meters) / Tasks

Distance & Tasks Chart

Area: _____   Date: _____

Distance (feet/meters) / Tasks

Distance & Tasks Chart

Area: _____   Date: _____

Distance (feet/meters) / Tasks

Distance & Tasks Chart

Area: _____   Date: _____

Distance (feet/meters) / Tasks

Distance & Tasks Chart

Area: _____ Date: _____

Distance (feet/meters) / Tasks

www.enna.c
www.productivitypres

Distance & Tasks Chart

Area: _____   Date: _____

Distance (feet/meters) / Tasks